# view from the top of the FERRIS WHEEL

poems by saraeve fermin

Clare Songbirds Publishing House Chapbook Series

ISBN 978-1-947653-14-6

The View from the Top of the Ferris Wheel © 2017 SaraEve Fermin

All Rights Reserved. Clare Songbirds Publishing House retains right to reprint.

Permission to reprint individual poems must be obtained from the author who owns the copyright.

Printed in the United States of America
FIRST EDITION

**Clare Songbirds Publishing House Mission Statement:**
Clare Songbirds Publishing House was established to provide a print forum for the creation of limited edition, fine art from poets and writers, both established and emerging. We strive to reignite and continue a tradition of quality, accessible literary arts to the national and international community of writers, and readers. Chapbook manuscripts and art quality poetry broadsides are carefully chosen for their ability to propel the expansion of art and ideas in literary form. We provide an accessible way to promote the art of words in order to resonate with, and impact, readers not yet familiar with the siren song of poets and writers. Clare Songbirds Publishing House espouses a singular cultural development where poetry creates community and becomes commonplace in public places.

**Clare Songbirds Publishing House**
140 Cottage Street
Auburn, New York 13021
www.ClareSongbirdspub.com

# Contents

| | |
|---|---:|
| For You | 9 |
| Brother/ Side Note | 10 |
| Firsts | 12 |
| All Things Unsaid | 13 |
| Talking to Ghosts | 15 |
| My Mother's Closet | 16 |
| Conversations with my Mother in Waiting Rooms, 2013 | 18 |
| The Elephants UnApology | 19 |
| Let's Never Come Back Here | 20 |
| What You Call One Thing I Call Another | 21 |
| Digging Out The Honey Pot | 22 |
| Fiona Apple's Parting Advice For Every 'I Know I Said Forever, But' | 24 |
| The Epileptic Monitoring Unit | 27 |
| Coney Island | 28 |
| Sitting in a Waiting Room, Rubbing Elbows | 30 |
| Ways to Love a Women with a Broken Brain | 31 |
| The Disability Joke | 32 |
| Conversations With The Young Cashier at the Express Lane, 2014 | 34 |
| Circus Freak | 36 |
| Spit | 37 |
| The Fight | 38 |
| Oatmeal Cookie Relapse | 39 |

| | |
|---|---|
| This Poem Got Drunk | 40 |
| After | 41 |
| All This You Can't Leave Behind | 42 |
| Having my Neuroses Over For Dinner | 43 |
| When I Say 'Depression' I Mean | 44 |
| When The Prescription Changes | 45 |
| Advice For The Clinically Stuck in Life | 46 |
| Me With Ice Cream Cone, Age 16 | 47 |
| Alternate Names for Oldest Daughter | 49 |
| Dinner, 1901 West Street | 50 |
| Life Unfulfilled | 53 |
| A Decade of Discontent | 54 |
| Easter Sunday | 57 |

*For Michael, Christine and Corissa,
I am sorry you keep dying in the stories.
Thank you for being the mirror.*

Thank you to the following publications for giving homes to this poems, or earlier versions of them. Gratitude.

*All Things Left Unsaid* and *For My Brother, an Apology* first appeared in Transcendence Magazine

*Digging Out The Honey Pot* and *Talking to Ghosts* first appeared in Free Verse Summer 2013 Vol. 2

*Conversations with my Mother in Waiting Rooms 2013* first appeared in Ghost House Review

*Conversation with the Young Cashier at the Express Lane 2014* first appeared in Swimming With Elephant's 'Light As A Feather' Anthology

*Circus Freaks* first appeared in Borderline

*A Decade of Discontent* first appeared in Red Paint Hill

*What You Call One Thing I Call Another, The Epileptic Monitoring Unit* first appeared in *WordsDance*

*Fiona Apple's Parting Advice For Every 'I Know I Said Forever, But-'* first appeared in *GERM Magazine*

*The Disability Joke* first appeared in Drunk In A Midnight Choir

The poem 'All This You Can't Leave Behind' contains the lyric 'This is fact not fiction/for the first time in years' by Death Cab For Cutie, A Lack of Color *Transatlanticism* 2003

Cover art and design by Stephanie Lane Sutton

Gratitude to the following people for their part in making this body of work come together, both directly and indirectly. These poems would not exist without the sparkle, guidance and encouragement of: Victor Armooh, Jozy Bentley, Gretchen R. Bouliane, Jason Carney, Sierra DeMulder, Stevie Edwards, Megan Falley, Thomas Fucaloro, Ginna Funk Wallace, Rose Gallant, Ayla and Helen Grebe Tricia Price Henley, Jennifer E. Hudgens, Natalie E. Illum, William James, Michael Jasso, Theron Jenkins, Karen G. , Victoria Kaloss, Erin Karcher, Elena Lee, Ryk McIntyre, Rachel McKibbens and Family, Mindy Nettifee, Michelle Nimmo, Amanda Oaks, Angelique Palmer, Chris Rockwell, Caroline Rothstein, Jon Sands, Nathan Say, Cecily Schuler, Mark Sniadecki, Stephanie Lane Sutton, Rachel Therres and Jeanann Verlee. New Jersey and New York for opening their venues to my voice.
Amanda Purn, my person, and her loving family.
Dr. Stephen Karceski, Epileptologist and Dr. Robert Goodman, Neurosurgeon, for saving me.
My mother, who washed the glue out of my hair every post-hospital stay.
Every bus and train ride I've endured, every cross country trip that made hours of writing and this book possible.
The witches of Pink Door, for the permission.


Louis and Oliver, I love you. We are the Fantastic Foxes.

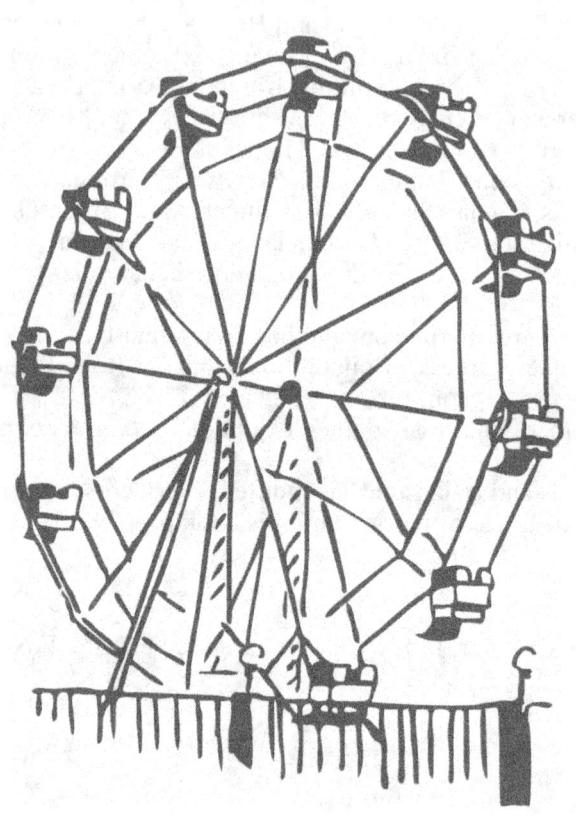

## For You

*After Megan Falley*

For You, bone dry water fountains,
stars that never shoot. Days where
the rain seems like only a flood.
A woman who colors only in the lines,
a dozen peas under your mattress.

For you, sticky sweet drippings
to lap from broken wine casks,
empty prescription bottles,
dry hypodermics crunching beneath
your bare feet. Only Disney villains,
only darkened nightlights.
Row after row of unblinking
Christmas lights, kicked in Jack-O-Lanterns.

For you, outdated maps and expired batteries,
never change for the bus and unending blisters,
a drawer full of mismatched socks.

For you, chocolate cake on your birthday,
year after year after year.

For you, a dead canary's murder,
elaborate shoebox funeral tuned
uncontrollable night terror

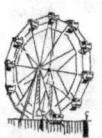

## Brother/Side Note

*So now we say goodnight*
*From our own separate sides*
*Like brothers on a hotel bed.*
   - Death Cab for Cutie

You are all grown up now,
little brother in a man's body.
Only a few apartments away from me,
yet farther than you've ever been
in our entire lives.

Side-note: blood that has been diluted
too many times with gin and tobacco
will run just as quickly as water.

Yesterday I thought I spotted you
in our apartment complex parking lot
and felt my body lock with a thick fisted fury,
felt my throat burn with all the ugly
I am tempted to scratch into your car door.

Side-note: I am Harley Quinn
without her makeup,
her laughter, her bombs.

I sat beside you in that intake office,
witnessed you unzip your burlap mask of sarcasm,
remained stoic as confessed dreams
of wrapping your new Nissan around an oak tree
on the way home from work.

Side-note: You live faster than
most roller coasters.

I try to tell myself this all comes from
an inconsolable part pigeonholed purple rage
youth that I was never able to reach,
the hand I always grasped for
while crossing the street,
the hands that now cannot still themselves
long enough to hold my own during a seizure.

Now you play with the rings on your fingers,
too big,
I imagine melting them down to silver slugs,
putting one between the eyes of the wolf
that haunts your mind.
I want to be the one to put the monster down,
want to know I can still talk you off cliffs.

Instead, that night I drove home and ached
for my baby brother

Side-note: If you are the wolf
and I am the witch,
I have read enough fairy tales to know
this cannot end well.

When they lock you away,
 it will not be in a tower.
I am enough Fairy Tale to know
this is how it always goes with family.

I am enough Harley Quinn to not know
how to stop loving the wicked.

Side-note: The ones we love
never die an easy death.

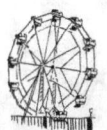

# Firsts

*After Jeanann Verlee*

His best friend. His protector. His call for help.
His *always knows I'm gonna give in.* His money to do
his homework. Him, quarters fed into the arcade game.
Him, not coming home yet. Him, my responsibility.
His dead canary. His first funeral. His can't eat alone
during lunch period. Him, Irish Twin. Him, paid
quarters to get off this back. His best friend. His tend
to forget. His past. His easy life. His own room.
His locked door. His privacy. His privilege.
His first drink, Bacardi. His first hair dye, red.
His first job, as your employee. His coming out.
His earnest fear. His grow up real fast. His moving
out.. His *please, try not to have a seizure in front of
me*. His can't take being in hospitals. Him, not being a
part of my recovery. Him, double standards. His drunk.
His doesn't have to call. His NYC life. His bipolar.
His nervous breakdown. Him, white from the sight of
blood. Him, hung over. His snort everything. His my
life is not your poetry. His not the same history. His
not the same trauma. His trauma. His nervous break-
down. His hands his get a job, get off the system, get
out. Him, two middle fingers. Him, tattooed and
angry. Him, push everyone away. His silence. His
trauma. His best friend. His recovery. Him, over
medicated at Thanksgiving. Him, slurred speech. Him,
12 steps. His nervous breakdown.. His confessions.
His laughter. His medications. His sister. His best
friend.
His sister

# Things Unsaid
*After M,M&J*

I'm sorry I wasn't born earlier. That there weren't enough years between us. I'm sorry that I came first, that I learned how to survive, that I needed it all for myself. I'm sorry that I was beat the hardest of us all, that your elephant tears always collected the holiest in her hands. I'm sorry we don't remember the same history, that you are in all the poems, but not—that you are always a bottle, or an empty chair, or a phone call, always disappointment. I'm sorry for giving your stories away, sorry that when you cried in the auditorium I was disgusted, sorry I killed you in my dreams— twice. I'm sorry our mother saw *Depression* only in you, sorry that my *sadness* is only a mood. I'm sorry I couldn't run fast enough from you, and then wanted only to be a part of your life. I'm sorry your boyfriends loved me, that you kept them from me. I'm sorry for all the doors I opened for you—the jobs, the conversations, I'm sorry that you are now best friends with my maid of honor, and that we don't talk anymore. I am sorry I never stopped you from hurting our sister, sorry I never took the knives away, sorry I let you play with matches. I'm sorry that I know there is honesty and a tiny core you keep to yourself, sorry that your broken hurts and I do not know how to fix it. I am sorry that I am always trying to climb inside you with my words, sorry that you always think that they are about you. Sorry I have seen you smile, have seen you without your beard and middle fingers. Sorry I dyed your hair, pierced your ears. I am sorry I took the pills they gave me, learned how to be quiet, I'm sorry I hid my scars. The truth is, I was always afraid, felt you slipping from me, even as I tried to shake you off like a piece of gum on a hot boardwalk. It's because of the way our mother taught us to walk to school—hands clasped, palm in palm. Every crossroad stretches out before me like a highway and my hand, it opens and closes on its own, looking for a ghost.

## Talking to Ghosts

I always pick up when she calls.
She knows this. It's why she refuses
to call after noon, the one rule

that never sticks, with her it is
all rules and I am always breaking
them, always breaking plates,

always breaking inside. I grew up in
the quietest house on the block, we
are all secrets here. I am best

at keeping them, have never called
the cops, have never called
Social Services have never really

told the truth. I learned early on
the authorities had no authority over
her empire, three children are easy

to grow if you have all the right
fixings. I'm still not fixed, still can't
get over the fact that I am in love with

rusted things, I can feel the secrets
beneath the peeling metal, bubbling to
the surface, once smooth structures

giving way to fine lines, cracking with age.
I have learned to crack so quietly,
you never even hear the skin pop.

She always calls in the morning.
I always answer.
Even if it's just her ghost.

## My Mother's Closet

My mother thinks I don't notice the way she has been growing
my grown-up closet. It seems

I can't leave her house without a beautiful new party dress
heaped upon me, like I am the plainest

cupcake in the display, vanilla, no frosting.
Or as if I've entered puberty all over again and

she's just *dying* to get me into that awful sunflower hat she
made me wear to my Junior prom.

We still argue over it to this day. Now,
we share the same style. Now she's passing down

dresses and skirts that she has owned for years.
My mother does not know how to shop for her

new body. When they took the cancer away
they took her breasts as well and at first

she was fine with that.
A proud alpha female and nudist at heart;

her breasts had done all they could do
for her four children, now they were

a cosmetic inconvenience.
She thought she would wake up hollowed, clean.

Instead reconstructive surgery, two saline bags, more chemo so
now she wears my outgrown bras,

her new frame makes everything that was once comfortable ill
fitting.

My mother insists I am all empire waists and dark colors, that
she will have to tuck in my tag as

I walk down the aisle. She does not listen when
I tell her I don't want chiffon and lace laden

wedding, I dream of linen and sand in my toes. I've tried giving her some tips, what it's like to

wake up with an extra ten pounds on your chest. My mother tells me she has been living like that

ever since the first diagnosis, the disintegrating cartilage in that crawled up and down her spine,

worse than cancer but not, still invading and eating her alive. My mother hands me a new dress

she ordered for herself that does not fit, and I am angry with her.

I don't want to feel like I am collecting the item of a dead woman, like I am amassing a wardrobe

full of shells shed disguised in blues and greens, this ocean of a woman I've never learned how to

receive, only how to drown in. My mother shows me her emptying closet.

Tells me that the heaviest weight is the ones you don't see.

## Conversations with my Mother in Waiting Rooms, 2013

On the way to the oncologist,
my mother confesses she just wants
to give up already. Silently

I become the selfish one for
hating the drug that I am losing
my family to one form at a
time, for hating the drug that
has broken her down from
heavy-footed panic inducing

childhood terror to the shuffling
stooped wreckage she is now. I am
the selfish one who won't let her go.

See, we poets don't get to kill our parents;
ask Plath, ask Sexton, ask Olds. We
just clean up the aftermath. Now, all

she ever talks about are the good
days and bad days. Pain on a scale
from one to ten. My mother is a fifty

year old woman trapped in crumbling
sand castle of a body. On the car ride home,
she tells me she does not want to live anymore.

I don't respond; let her think I've been stunned into silence,
that my response has been stolen by the rushing wind, my
own defective neurons. Truth is, there is a certain grace in
accepting the inevitable.

## The Elephant's UnApology

My family deals in spite.
We take our coffee with blood,
the words *motherfucke*r are never
far from my lips.

This is the legacy I have been given.
A ravenous fury, a furnace where a belly
belongs and a sparkplug mouth.
We've always been comfortable playing

in puddles of gasoline,
or favorite game growing up was
*duck duck you take the blame this time, ok?*
We were three kids against one.

My mother can't not refer to us as *you guys*,
as if she bore me and my siblings simultaneously,
like we are a hand, the fingers pulling her apart.

She is always the victim in these stories.
The truth is, I have felt both love and hate from
her in equal parts, and that is what makes the
killing that much harder.

This is how I learned to love the monster.
Through a fish eye lens. Always with one eye
on the door. The way the elephant loves the
circus—because it is the only place it does not

make too much noise. My family loves like a
circus. Vagabond. Like this heart is a train,
they jump on and off, and I am in the last car,
trunk waving, clutching a white flag.

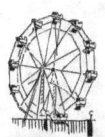

## Let's Never Come Back Here

"Can you keep a secret?
I'm trying to organize
a prison break"
Bob Harris, *Lost In Translation*


We are karaoke at midnight.
Closing down bars over outdated drinks,
always Gin.
Watching the sunrise over
freshly picked apples.

# What You Call One Thing I Call Another
*After Cristin O'Keefe Apotwitz*


In my defense, a poet once told me 'poets make the best liars.' In my defense, I slept with a painting of jesters above my childhood bed. In my defense, the painted lady and the razor in hand.

No, he never pried me open; never saw the blade fall from my fingertips. That was my truth. Still, I saved the best of myself for him—when the anxiety of lying with a woman who loved him began to soak through his clothing, I reassured him in kinder tones than I have ever used on myself. I was not a sin, I was a celebratory feast and he was no gentleman. He was a hungry fool with the meat of his last kill still hanging from his teeth. *Wipe your fucking mouth.* I said. The mistake was letting him think I was prey. The mistake was letting him think he chose me.

In my defense, my favorite rides are the ones that spin you around the fastest. In my defense, I love when the floor drops out. In my defense, I will take second place if it means being your first runner up.

Distance does not make us stronger, does not make us safer. It breaks down lies so that they are digestible by the time they reach the other party. I have loved harder apparitions that I have never met the ghosts of people's quickly whispering fingers. I am a collection of late night confession and open door dreams, find myself attracted to old souls and wandering stars. When you allow the dreams of married men to unfold into your miles away life, when you start to drink just so you can turn your computer on, when the insomnia creeps in, know you have simply become a placeholder. It's time to turn celebration. String memory from neuron to neuron like crepe paper and become welcome party to the grief.

In my defense, I've never met a carnival I could just walk away from. In my defense, I'll always read your letters. In my defense, I tattooed my wrist to keep it safe.

## Digging Out The Honey Pot

"The only lies for which we are truly punished are those we tell ourselves"
-V.S. Naipaul, *In a free State*

We love like children.
What I mean to say is,
we love without
consequence.
We love when
no one is looking,
tell ourselves this is a truth.

It isn't.
It is pulling rabbits out of a hat.
The type of easy magic
children love.
What I mean to say is,
we're better tugging at wool
than telling the truth.

We hide behind the guise of
*poetry*. Metaphors are easy lies.
We are painters of our own
stupid futures. We are not getting
any younger.
What I mean to say is
we have been playing this game
for endless years and my arms
hurt from reaching,
my knuckles
hurt from lack of contact
my teeth hurts from swallowing
you back in small bites,
trying to assimilate to your apathy.

This kind of love, it gives
poetry a bad name, this kind of love
is too many mosquito bites and no
salve, it is the thick roof of August
heat that settles on your lungs and
makes walking away difficult. It is
the kind of love that comes with a
pocketful of good excuses.

What I mean to say is, I will never
be a good liar, but you bring out
the best magician in me. Truth is,
I've got a backyard full of dead rabbits
and all my hats have holes in them.

## Fiona Apple's Parting Advice for Every 'I Know I Said Forever, But--'

She is teaching me to play the piano,
says this is the last thing she has for me.
But I am all left-handed, emotional,
banging on the sharps and flats.

Still, she gets me. We are both run on sentences, bitter
highs and baby doll lows.
She knows why I only write when I'm sad.

She knows that I don't live in the gray, i
t's where I go to remember myself.
That I always come back.
She does not stop me, or ask me
to change any of my bad habits,
not when I flick the lighter and inhale,
not when I bite my nails, not when I
cry for the entire weekend and forget
to return her calls,

start taking antidepressants instead,
not even when she has to pull me out
of the medication like a drunk from a bar.

She sees the apocalypse in me,
slips a pencil in my hand, only stops my railing
against the wood and ivory long enough to make notes:

*Here is where he promises you forever.*
*Here is where he makes you say it first.*
Like an Ativan slipped under the tongue,
 she will not let me go, and I know
she is with me now, hands over mine,
breath in ear.
*Here is where she never smiles back,*
*all the times you bit your lower lip.*

I am working the foot pedals,
all twelve years of musical instruction
come flooding back,
like my hands never left an instrument,
my lips crack.
I chalk up time signatures, crazy ones
no partner will ever be able to follow
and Fiona, she is laughing now
at the abandon of it all.

We are both laughing with
the dizzying graveyard orchestra
love has left us to dance alone in.

*Here is where he says return the favor.*
*Here, where he insists he is right.*

*Here is the fading ink of his letters, the house*
*you both built blowing away board by board.*

When I know it's almost done,
and the red fog lifts off my shoulders

and I'm back to an easy waltz,
she leans over, whispers:
*Here is where you tell him* **enough**.
*Here is where you say apology not accepted.*

*Here is where you say mine,*
*beautiful me.*

When the music stops, she is gone,
taking the terrible with her.

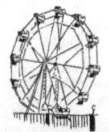

## The Epileptic Monitoring Unit

*And every single fight's alright/with my brain*
*I just want to feel everything*
*~Fiona Apple*

The 6am car rides. The piercing, promise of the clear blue sky and another day wasted. The GWB. The 12 dollar toll. The 25 dollar parking lot. Columbia Presbyterian Hospital, O, Castle of Miserable, of clinical depression, my twenties and staggering convulsions of darkness. $8^{th}$ floor, Neurology, The Epileptic Monitoring Unit, with its polished hardwood hallway floors that no patient could appreciate, tethered to the wall by a tangle of electronics, sanctioned to the bed by guard rail for safety, emergency cords and alarms. Home of the wires, the glue, the air guns, the always acetone smell. The crying children, the pulled hair, their haggard mothers praying over their sleeping bodies. The hall always whispering with 24 hour cameras, transfers, the whirring and clicking of the CT scans, the burn of nuclear medicine. The acronyms: PET scans, SPECTS scans, WADA test, VNS implant. No privacy, a tendency to seize in the bathroom, *Sorry, we're short staffed, we have to help who we can get to first.* View of the Hudson; same room twice irony, summers smell like stale air conditioning and hospital cleaner, all the meals boiled and never quite reaching my mouth. IV in my left arm. Can't write. Bruises, nausea, withdrawal, the pounds lost, shaved head, the steel spike migraines. Readmissions. The first DNR. Always Fox News. Vonnegut dies. 15 doctors a day and always alone. My mother asleep in a chair, no spare pillows making do for 19 days and always alone. Keeping myself up flipping through the same 13 channels at 2 AM, watching American Gladiators reruns, laughing at what we thought was strong because sleep deprivation, alone. Fifth medication failure asking God why and getting no response, alone. Recurring nightmares surgical steel shining and MRI backlit, alone. My now husband there every day, holding my hand every time I go into the dark, every time I lose consciousness. Still there are no words for lungs that clench closed, a throat that fills with concrete, the words *I love you* frozen in a mind that only hears ringing, sees colors as my brain give into the misfiring electrical current running it rampant. I go into every seizure always. Alone.

## Coney Island

Things no one tells you about bringing home the lost and
found mermaid—

You bought the 50 pound bag of sand,
kiddie pool complete with slide, did the
research on proper saline and chlorine levels
to keep me comfortable.

Would not let the dog nibble on my tail,
brought me new bikini tops, as if I would forget
about the fishing lure scars river marking my torso,
forever land locking me to you.


It was only when the blue in my eyes faded to grey
that you asked me what was missing.

To love me you must grow an ocean.
My heart beats like a mollusk opening and closing,
waiting for the perfect grain of sand to land on its tongue
and begin to grow iridescent bubble,

my heart is all gravity and pin bones,
all grenade and shrapnel imploded,
ill-fitting in this chest
where they forgot to slice me a set of gills

I have been trying to correct this anatomical fault ever since.
I never meant to become  a landmine of a body,

To love me, imagine the air being drawn out of your lungs;
imagine your body crumpling like a sheet of paper in the
hands of a God invisible.

You must understand that I am willing to commit small suicide rather than endure this cycle of malfunction,

Would rather face an oxygen deprived death than
remember the sound of my own being stolen from me.

This is how mermaids are caught,
 the warmth of the sun too seductive
on their salt burned skin,
swimming too close to the surface,
we are mistaken for manatees,
you must understand why this never gets any easier.

So if you can never love me,
If I become more maintenance than majesty,

If I become all encompassing,

turn out to be a Coney Island wash up
instead of your Disney Princess Ariel,

You must understand when it comes to survival—

Nothing should be taken personally

## Sitting in a Waiting Room, Elbow Rubbing

Like the time I said
*This will last forever*
and the time they said
*This will only hurt a minute*

   Like the time I told you
   I would never do it again
   and the time they told me
   *This will make it better*

      Like the time I told you
         *This is my heart*
         and the time they told me
         *This is what's wrong*

I love you,
like a seizure.
I cannot be stopped.
I am a spot on a scan,
slowly spinning myself brighter
until you have not choice—
but to give in.

# Ways to Love a Woman with a Broken Brain
*after William James*


1. Do not ask about her past. When it spills out at the worst times—crowded train stations, anniversary dinners, while separating the whites at the laundry mat—do not try to stuff it back in. She will confess like the floor dropping out, so learn to walk tightrope, to appreciate the ground; you will crave gravity the way she grabs for a prescription bottle.

2. Do not ask about the prescription bottles, how they brick the room closed, how she clings to them like the saints of bad manners. Do not reprimand her when she falls "off schedule", understand why drying out of this fog is necessary, even if it means a weekend of uncontrolled emotions. Do not stuff her back into these bottles; there will be days when you will have to coax her out of them.

3. Do not trust any emotion you have to coax out of her. She was raised on drunken confessions, she is at her most honest when she is white hot , out of control, a fountain of emotion and erupting truths. No amount of pleading can pull this honesty out of her. Silence is a measured practice.

4. Do not trust the silence. When she falls into the darkest nights and still cannot seem to sleep, when the daytime drinking starts, when she cuts off her own hair, ask way. This is not the time for reflection. Smother her in attentive concern.
5. Do not ask about the bruises, the scars, the razor. This is a personal hell she is fighting her way out of, and it will be like trying to put out fire with rubbing alcohol—you will burn any bridge you had hopes of crossing. Her body is a warzone and she signed up for the long haul. None of it has been a mistake; they are all stops along the path that has made her.

6. Do not assume the scars are a want for dying. Do not ask about any of her apocalypse, it is not a burning. She will break and rebuild herself before the end. Do not call her phoenix; she is not flight risk or bonfire beauty. She is tempered. She knows the trick to swallowing swords. You just open wide.

## The Disability Joke
*After Patricia Lockwood*

The disability joke is that you were travelling alone, travelling halfway across the country for the first time.

The joke is this was a lot of firsts for you—first train ride, first time travelling across time zones, first time travelling without a trained seizure companion.

The disability joke is that you felt really free.
The joke is you were taking a train because you would not fly without your husband, and you could not find a dog sitter, so your husband stayed home with the dog so you took a thirty hour train.

The disability joke is that you have epilepsy. You've had a brain surgery and traumatic brain injury resulting in partial blindness. You also have aphasia, which is the same as words being locked in your head, which, if you are a poet, is the same as running in circles drunk. The joke is your stubborn pride, who will not allow you to get a blind cane, even though that would unlock a world of questions you would not need to answer anymore.

The joke gets funnier when you buy a 'disability ticket' for your train ride and find out it is not good for anything. Admit it, you see it coming. Or maybe you don't, maybe you are partially blind like me. After all, it's just neurodiversity, right?

The disability joke is waiting for you in Chicago. It is not the transfer, not the eight hours of dead time or worrying about your luggage. It is the conductor who is everything you've dreamed about—one hand on the railing, one foot on the platform, navy blue suit, the yellow stripes and tie, so much like a cop. Still, the joke shoots out of his mouth when you ask for directions and he says, *Please take a seat upstairs.*

The disability joke does not care that you are a liability to Amtrak. It does not care that you have gone out of your way to purchase a disability ticket to make this ride safe for yourself and for others. It does not care that when you have a seizure, your right arm postures, becomes so stiff you once took a door out of its frame because your hand locked on it as you went down. The joke does not care that you do everything you can to be safe for yourself and others.

The disability joke, dressed as a conductor, stifles your protests

and tells you there are no more reserved seats so you find a seat upstairs. It does not care that the bathrooms are downstairs  The joke does not know you suffer from kidney stones and drink about three gallons of water a day, and that being near a bathroom is a necessity. The joke does not care that you will now be required to walk down *stairs* on a moving train. The joke looks at you and sees a normal woman. *Someone who can pass*. The joke thinks that it does not discriminate, that it is being an upstanding citizen when it lets you and other visibly disabled people do things all on your own. The joke claps itself on the back when you and your friends do well with your disability poems, thinks, *Wow, if only I had something like that to write about*. It goes home and writes *The Theory of Everything. Silver Lining Playbook. Rain Man. Fight Club. Girl Interrupted*. Admit it. Even the joke shakes it's head at itself sometimes.

The disability joke comes with a punch line. It's so funny, you never forget it. When your husband calls Amtrak and insists they switch your seat, when he goes through all the wasted breath of explaining that epilepsy *is* a movement disorder and that you did go through all the precautions of making this a safe trip, the attendant will say to him, *And she is travelling alone like that*? You will carry the weight of this accusation; you will fold it up and place it in the back of your mind with every other archaic lie about your disease that has been fed to you.

Even the disability joke knows that was going too far.

The disability joke is that you slept in the sun car so you would not hurt anyone. Even in your discomfort, 15 hours into your train ride, you were thinking of others, and how to make yourself smallest.

The joke is you are not afraid of having a seizure on stage but rather of having one in the audience and interrupting something beautiful.

Is disability ever funny? Not in the 12 year old, call your friend a 'retard' way. I get more compliments on my sarcasm about my disability than when I try to crack a joke-- What does that say about me, about the joke?

The joke laughs. The joke believes that archaic myth, that people with epilepsy will swallow their tongue, thinks that I am unconscious and tells it's friends 'that girl should not be in public' when I interrupt the checkout line at CVS with my drop and convulsions, thinks I cannot hear the horror masked as concern in her tone. Thinks I will not remember it and be afraid to leave my own house for the next decade.

## Conversations with the Young Cashier at the Express Lane 2014

In one hand I have a pint of Ben and Jerry's
strawberry ice cream, the other, oatmeal
cookies. These are my tools, I am a fucking

artist of the ice cream sandwich. The cashier
is seventeen years old, pierced lip, heavy eyeliner,
shock of red hair.

Size 8 and heavy on a diet of self-loathing, trying
to find herself in the quiet dismissal of others.
She looks me up and down and in a half second

I see the world at seventeen again, think myself
invincible, think myself able to take without giving back,
think that I can laugh at the thought of ever

letting myself reach 269 pounds,
as if I were immune to the slow progression
of time and genetics.

I knew how to fit into social norms, how to swallow stones,
how to use my body as admission
to clubs I didn't know existed yet. I was

seventeen and I was invincible,
my failure to see statistics as more than math
becoming my downfall.

The cashier looks at my purchases, gives me
a slow eye roll, thinks I do not notice. I spend
most of my days grinding my teeth,

preparing for young ladies like this one.
I am a shock to their system, not afraid to admit
that I am more turned on by a ripe to bursting

sticky sweet cherry pies glossy pocket cookbook
than any half naked man
flashing across Extra Magazine.

She rings up my purchases and I want to tell her to dance,
to do things now that her body will not allow her
to do when she is older.

I want to make her a badass ice cream sandwich
and ask her all the questions someone should have asked me
when I was her age: what she is reading,

if the boys in her school call her a slut,
how she really feels about the teacher who is
undoing her father's abandonment  and tell her

the ugly feeling in her gut is real.
But I was seventeen once, and I remember
what it is like when your head is full of paychecks,

football games and calorie counting, exams,
hiding her scale, getting to work on time.
I want to tell her I was seventeen once too.

That all of the magazine at the express
checkout aisle warned me about this future.
I hope that she sees it coming better than I did.

## Circus Freaks

When you tell someone you love
you are going to run away and join the circus,
their first reaction should not be
"but you are allergic to cats."

You began to recite a laundry list of reasons why
this was not an optimal career choice for me.
My fear of heights meant I would never ride the elephants
and the fact that I always cut myself while shaving
was a sign of unsteady hands
that would never grace the trapeze bars.

I've never been good at two truths and a lie,
I wear my past like a Siamese twin,
speak in tongues and have an uncanny knack
for pulling the High Priestess from the deck.
I walk tightropes daily and have contorted myself
into what passes for happiness,
my scars a down payment for what I try to predict.

I was not looking for absolution
when I told you my biggest fear
was that the strong man would break his back
under the weight of all my insecurities, t
he crack echoing through the silent tent
as the audience sat slack jawed
and breathless.

I've grown weary of waiting for traveling carnivals,
my talent is not a vessel for reality television.
I leave no forwarding address
but the next time you see me,
my head will be inside the lion's mouth.

I was never allergic to cats.  You should have known better.

## Spit

She is so, so frail right now,
china dolls are built army strong around her.
Still, inside is always this disgust,
this suck it up,
the part of her that reins in every last tear and
does not allow the last wave to pass over her,
the bone ache shudder of a person who has fought
rib cracking thunder boxing matches for 15 rounds.
Come away a kicked dog and cried,
cried simply at the loss of it all

# The Fight

This is what the body does. Skin grows back and nails do too. Even if we spend fifty dollars a week sculpting it into something sharp, angular, maybe turquoise this week, with glittering accents. Our hair will never Barbie itself into permanence so we take instruments to it, the ones regularly seen in horror films. Chop or shave or slice or smooth or pluck or buzz or trim or burn. The list goes on and on, but hair will show up in places unwanted, will silver beneath our scalps and sprout, pushing our painted tresses skyward. and waterfall. Our manes will lose their radiant pride and we will return to status quo. This is what the body does. Starts out so soft, you can feel the place where the skull is still forming beneath a newborns ethereal head. We are not even fully formed when pushed into this world. The body takes care of the rest, connects. Bone reaches towards bone and fuses and this is what happened later on, when older bones are broken and reset, when skin is split, blood rushes to the surface to come together, to make us whole again. The body keeps fighting even when the skin is split by one's own hand. The body keeps growing back, keeps rejecting, keeps showing up each day, even if the brain is drowning in last night's alcoholic mess. Even if the feet burn from running from everything that hurts, the body will callous, will scab and peel and new skin will appear. Even beneath the muddle of medications, the brain struggles to string words together, you sit down to task and form sentences. Neurons die but new ones form and you fight, fill notebook after notebook, turn trauma to bedtime story. The body will continue to do its job. It's up to you to do the rest of the work

## Oatmeal Cookie Relapse

At a party, he declares anyone who is triggered
by an oatmeal cookie needs serious help.

I bite my tongue, blood sweeter than any
chocolate kiss. I know that I have given him the
benefits of the doubt just one too many times,

thinking that the poet in him will at least
make up for his lack of sympathy towards
What might seem like a trivial issue, or a feminist stance.
This has never been a feminist stance, never about birth control
or lack of tampons at the pharmacy.
This is me talking about my closest hurt.

This is me skinning the meat off the bones
for a room full of poets, wanting them to see
the mess involved in becoming the skeleton.
It is not pretty, like dissolving,

it is bleeding cuticles and sleepless nights,
growling stomach and waiting for your next meal.
It is broken resolve and the same New Years' Resolution
year after year after year.

It is knowing certain road trips are that much more anticipated
when a Cracker Barrerl or Wawa stop is a part of the itinerary,
the time the package of Girl Scout cookies disappeared
into your grief during an episode of *Six Feet Under*,
 it is a quiet panic 400 miles from you home when you realize

you did not pack the good tweezers, locked in the
bathroom of a room you share with eight other people,
examining everything you want to undo about yourself.

Why can't I have my cookies and my rage
and the body I want too?
This is not a feminist stance; it is not calling it
relapse this is saying a poem about oatmeal cookies was
enough to trigger a six hour rant. What do you call it?

## This Poem Got Drunk-

and proclaimed
*I love you like drowning.*
to all the empty streets while
stumbling home.

Everyone who was woken up that night
sees this as a sign
of a sinking ship marriage
but the truth is,

I love you.
Like drowning,
going under without the
one thing that means
the world to me.

l:ike walking
for miles along the shore,
music in ear, shell in pocket,
and catching your eye.

the art of finding a man
who can so easily flatten
my ego.

I love you,
like drowning.
Like the only thing left to do
is let go and breathe you in

## After

After all the prayers, and the meditation.
the unsent letters to the mourned. Yourself.

After you've put the paint and the nursery
decorations up. After your mother asks if

she should give the crib and changing table
to your sister. After you start bleeding again.

After you've moved your master bed
to the nursery floor like an anxious child

on Christmas Eve. After you put only one
thing on that Christmas list. A name.

After you realize this is not a matter of chance.

### All This You Can't Leave Behind

Your last thought are important Claire.
They're all you get to take with you. –Nina, *Cake*

Indigo twilight, and the ribbon of orange-gold that rims the horizon. Ben and Jerry's Late Night Snack Ice Cream. My baby sister's gap toothed smile, the first day of summer, holding hands and jumping into the pool. I'd give anything to get that back. *'This is fact not fiction, for the first time in years...'* The time I travelled to Boston by myself. Swedish Fish candies. The way every venue feels before a reading— so many words ready to dance off tongues like ballerinas off diving boards in full costume, unscripted. Stephen King's *The Shining*. All of my tattoos, shimmering on my ghostly silhouette. The wind chimes he bought me for our first apartment. The first dip on my favorite roller coaster, the swings at sunset. Purple hair dye. My favorite carousel horse, the one that went into the ocean during the hurricane. The best and worst poem that I ever write. Lavender. Leroi's Pennywhistle solo at the end of 'Bartender'. Sugar Daddy Caramel Pops. A set of faerie wings, in case I am afraid to fly.
One more night with my wolf pack, I promise not to fall asleep this time…

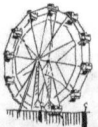

## Having My Neuroses Over For Dinner

It starts out the smallest table; I've set it just for two.
My guest he holds my hand, tells me it's ok,
to just get it off my chest,
I've been so strong, and I have to laugh.
It starts out as a word small enough
to fit in my mouth but then I start to choke.
The waiters I have not ordered come over
and ask my guest if he would like a drink a
nd I begin to spit up ocean, but the waiters,
they do not pay attention, not even when
they are standing in ankle high water,
not even when tiny pirate ships
begin crashing against their calves,
creating mayhem in my kitchen.
My guest, he ask to be excused to the bathroom and I shrug,
look like a water fountain
and the waiters are snickering.
When he leaves I shoot the waiters a dirty look
but they are all behind glass walls,
ones I have only now realized need to be cleaned.
I cough, try to push the water out,
get the word off my tongue
but scales come up, and I panic,
can feel the tip of a fishhook. My guest comes back,
it's too late for me to try and grab the hook.
I sit on my hands,
but it's no use, they keep coming up to my face,
looking for something to grab on to,
I keep looking for a pressure valve, some release,
I don't know where this tiny roaring Atlantic is coming from.
My guest puts on his waders, calls for the check.
*Honestly, honey, you just gotta breathe.*
He says, reeling the line.

## When I Say Depression, I Mean…

I'm only eating so people will stop asking
questions. I forgot to refill the medications,
oh well. The dog vomited in the bed, so I just
covered it up and went back to sleep. I mean sleep
as a lifestyle. Curtains always drawn. The beige
comforter, the white crochet blanket, the cotton
sheets so much like the hospital. The perfume you
stopped using after the surgery changed the way it
smelled. I mean peanut butter three times a day
because protein. I mean the calendar on the wall
says 2003 but it's 2015, and the poems won't come
anymore, or the all make you sound So Sad.
Lonely. Abused. Crazy. Defective. Like they took
this brain of yours apart but were never able to put
it back together. I mean Humpty Dumpty. I mean
oh well, so sad. I mean I mean *fine* is your favorite
word. I mean *woman*. Inherited. Time bomb.
Flight risk. Bear claw hammer scream nightmares,
smiles for the camera. If you ask me,
*I'll do it tomorrow, or tomorrow, or tomorrow…*

## When the Prescription Changes

from *twice a day* to **take as needed** /and my hands start to shake/ I am not ready for this responsibility/ the only other option/ is to admit there is a sharp thing/ deep inside of me that I do not know/ how to throw away/ the poet on stage/ who is a full decade younger than me/ says he is too old to still be taking about blood/ about scars/ about the sharp thing inside of him that will not die/ not knowing how to say/something inside of me is breaking/ I think of the pills/deep in my bag/ the new safety blanket/ I think of wine/ how many glasses I need to drink/ before I stop recognizing my handwriting/ I think of his bad excuses/ how he didn't want to be another target for my sad/ didn't want to get any blood on his collar/ and trail me into his home/ all this responsibility/ that he is not ready for/ like a boy who mows down a fawn/ without the decency/ of hauling the body to the side of the road/who just keeps driving/ whistling into his wide open future

## Advice for the Clinically Stuck in Life

*After Stevie Edwards*

Buy the ticket. Skip the meal. Save the pennies.
Return the dress. Kiss all the strangers. Don't stop dancing, your body will tell you when you've had enough. Rip everything open like it is a present on Christmas morning. Wake up the Gods. Hide your smile when they make you work for love. Kill your ghosts. All of them. Drown the phone. Write over your scars, live in the veins running, running under them. Feel. Punch walls, break a fist. Wear red on your wedding day. Marry the ocean, it will always return. Fight and fuck loudly and with intent, get what you want. Throw the pennies down the well. Eat the cake alone on the kitchen floor at 2 am. Use the ticket, take a train. Be a stranger. Buy a new dress.

## Me With Ice Cream Cone, Age 16

Men crawl by in loud cars
just to catch a glimpse of
your slow swirling tongue.

The way you bring your lips
to the vanilla and kiss the chill
will dog their sleep, cause them

to thrust out in stiff-necked dreams.
Your lipstick on the napkin will become
some kitchen designer wall paper..

## Alternate Names for the Oldest Daughter

*After Danez Smith*

1. Indentured servant
2. Father's eyes, grandfather's suicide
3. First to exit womb but last to leave home
4. Stockholm syndrome
5. Parent's Day stand-in
6. Collector of stray hands and spilled rage
7. Two tally marks high on the left thigh
8. Reader of bedtime stories, always shining night light
9. Unwanted, unwanted, unwanted
10. Keeper of the dragon secrets
11. Baby bird pushed out, wings clipped
12. Shepherd of an unruly brood
13. Shipwreck on concrete while mom sloshed vodka in my baby pool
14. Gnawed fists and bloody stomach
15. Never done walking away
16. Always the wrong answer, even when just an echo

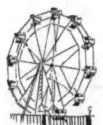

## Dinner, 1901 West St

In the beginning, there was only one poem about my
sister. This was when her bullshit was still novelty enough
that we could laugh over it at Christmas or a Birthday dinner.

This was when what *could* happen was still just a *could*,
when her life was hypothetical, when we used her both as
cautionary tale and relief valve,

*Hey Mom, remember the time*
*you caught Chrissy smoking*
*in the bedroom closet?*
*Where was she going to hide?*

In the beginning, I only had one family member
to write about, before the front door turned revolving.
Before everyone left, first my mind and then the house.
Before all the poems are really about me, and everyone hates
the costumes I stuff them in—the addict, the abusive,
the overeater—all reflections of myself.

Still, I am trying. I have learned how to cook a twenty pound
turkey. I know who in my family does not like onions, why
we don't bring wine to dinner.
I am the one who will bread and fry pile after pile of chicken
cutlet if that's what my siblings desire. Peel ten pounds of root
vegetables too, because everyone loves my mashed potatoes
the best.

This is how I was taught to love.
Over a full plate, laughing at the worst things that could
happen, letting time turn them into things we never could have
imagined surviving: Graduating high school homeless.
Your brother's car twisted up the median strip.
Taking your overdosing sister to the hospital.
The first seizure. The breast cancer.

Now, we scrape the ugly into the trash with the scrap. Get clean by rolling our sleeves up, turning the water as hot as possible, allow our hands to touch as we pass dripping plate to dishtowel to cupboard, return the serving platters and carving knives to their proper places in the decades old china cabinet that will one day be ours.

It's still astounds me, the way laughter always sounds childlike, echoing through a clean kitchen. How a little soap, salt water and time, can make you forgive almost anything.

## Life Unfulfilled

To believe you could wait for me, that our love
was train stations, a shared suitcase, prepaid ickets.
To believe that fevered whispers held the most truth.

To burrow, to look for you in all of my winter. It is
easiest to find your ghost in November, dancing with
my exhaled smoke under street lights, how can I make
you understand this, when you have cleaved me away
so cleanly? To believe that I'd know the smell of a wet
cornfield, to believe that you could teach me to find the
ocean in a thousand waving stalks. To believe I could
dry myself out, salt pillar silent and forget that I am all
water creature. to believe I could burn all of this down
and still have a place to call home, that reinvention was
never ending, to believe that if I continued to do it over
and over and over you would still recognize me, even
after the ugly, even after I used the worst word and the
silence, to believe that we would ever be the same after
the silence. To believe that I could cut myself open,
see myself bleed out before you, to believe you ever
had enough bandages to save me. To believe I wanted
to be saved. To believe was easier than to let your
ghost go.

# A Decade of Discontent

In the summer of my twenties
I was all ocean and broken,
having been cracked open like
an egg and reset like a timer,
I wanting the crash of the surf
against my spine to build me up.

When that failed I stopped swimming,
afraid I'd acquired a new density due to
the anchors gouged into my skull.
I read voraciously, took pictures as if
I knew a melancholy was coming,
gorged on sunshine and fresh air,
my blood preparing for the longest
winter.

Depression, when it comes, slips into
your bed like a warm cat on the coldest
North Eastern night, when you have been
fighting for too long, have been scraped raw
on all sides and are grateful for anything to hold
you.

Depression comes with its own routine and
rules, a quiet reassurance that your hole
will always be home, that you are accomplishing
something in the daily routine of burying
yourself in the grey.

When it takes over, it will not be a crutch,
you will tell yourself this is a new strength.

Depression will make the best story teller out of
your lies, you will not question when it starts
wearing your clothes, why it has convinced you
that wearing sweatpants all week is ok, or that
eating waffles and ice cream all week for dinner
is ok, or that not answering the phone for weeks ok,
depression will remind you deep down you
are still a broken child.

When you begin to wonder why you are letting
something takes up so much space in your mind
without charging rent, when it drives you to the
doctor, depression will be the knife at your throat,
threatening to spill blood if you spill the secrets of
your unspent decade.

The pills they will prescribe will be blue and round,
tiny lakes in the palm of your hand. A miracle magic
cure all. A wish granted.
Relief, when it is promised,
comes with a hidden clause, fine print.
It is why the Gods require we sign
all contracts in blood.
Pay our outstanding debts with life..

## Easter Sunday

It is Easter Sunday. Three generations of females occupy this two room apartment. It's the first time this has happened in over a decade. My younger sister who has spent most of this time in and out of rehab has finally found something she loved more than her PCP addiction—her now 9 month old daughter. I ask to hold my niece for the very first time. Up close, the baby's sucking is primal and I can understand why she was able to survive, why she is a beautiful lapful of giggles and snorts and elephant tears, why my sister is finally clean. Now my mother, she has the carved away body that I have always dreamed of. This is after the double mastectomy, back surgery and opiate addiction that has robbed her of her appetite. She gets through supper like a recovering anorexic, shuffling the food around her plate and promising me she will eat it later. But I know better. We all take turns reminding my youngest sister that she is not getting any younger and that she needs to lose some weight now, the words flying out of my mouth like something purged. My brother, my once best friend, is toeing the line between rock bottom and getting better by going cold turkey on all drugs, His waistline alone is enough to make me consider trying heroin and I am not saying that I am better than the rest of them; I am not saying that my books are not in the red in this sordid family tale. That night I will go home with my eating disorder firmly replanted. But it's on days like that I look at the family I come from, this stock, and then I remember, we are all just chasing a high.

SaraEve is a performance poet and epilepsy advocate from northeast New Jersey. A 2015 Best of the Net nominee, she has performed for both local and national events, including the 2013 Women of the World Poetry Slam, the Epilepsy Foundation of Greater Los Angeles 2015 Care and Cure Benefit to End Epilepsy in Children and as a reader for Great Weather for MEDIA at the 2016 NYC Poetry Festival on Governors Island. You might have met her volunteering at various national poetry slams. A Contributing Editor for Words Dance Magazine and Book Reviewer at Swimming with Elephants Publishing, her work can be found or is forthcoming in GERM Magazine, Drunk in a Midnight Choir, the Great Weather for MEDIA anthology *The Careless Embrace of the Boneshaker* and the University of Hell Press anthology *We Can Make Your Life Better: A Guidebook to Modern Living*, among others. Her first full length poetry anthology, *You Must Be This Tall to Ride,* was published by Swimming With Elephants Publishing in 2016. She believes in the power of foxes and self-publishing.
She loves Instagram: SaraEve41

www.ingramcontent.com/pod-product-compliance
Lightning Source LLC
Chambersburg PA
CBHW062040120526
44592CB00035B/1752